BRISBANE RIVER

History Guide by *CityCat* and *CityHopper*

1823-2023

David Gibson

with contribution by Dr Ray Kerkhove

This publication acknowledges the Traditional Owners of the waterway and surrounding lands traversed today. The introduction in 1996 of a CityCat service has provided new insights for both its citizenry and visitors to the city of Brisbane as to the ways in which a community evolved.

With few exceptions, each of the units of the CityCat fleet – of which there have been several generations – have been given an Indigenous name linked to locations on or overlooking the Brisbane River of today; names that provide an actual and subliminal understanding of the times before the arrival of the European when it was a place of hunting, fishing and games played. Examples include Tunamun (Petrie Bight), Gootcha (Toowong) and Mooroolbin (Hamilton sandbar).

For details of Indigenous camps in Brisbane refer to the book authored by Dr Ray Kerkhove – *Aboriginal Campsites of Greater Brisbane*, ISBN 9781925236521.

Published by
Boolarong Press
38/1631 Wynnum Road
Tingalpa Qld 4173
Australia.
www.boolarongpress.com.au

A catalogue record for this book is available from the National Library of Australia

ISBN: 9781922643674 (paperback)

Typeset in Garamond Premier Pro and Futura

Cover design by Boolarong Press

Printed and bound by Watson Ferguson & Company, Tingalpa, Australia

Contents

Map

The river system that today bisects Brisbane as the Capital City of Queensland was originally a steep Ice Age stream emptying 20 kms east of Amity Point (Moreton Bay being a plain). Then, 6,000 years ago, the seas rose, and the river broadened. First Nations people remember this as the Creator Carpet Snake (some say Eel or Bunyip) being chased down the Great Divide by Goanna, who was trying to steal her eggs. Her slithering gouged out the river. She carried her eggs in her mouth and spilled them out at Moreton Bay, where they became the islands and all the people. The river was also called Maiwar, which meant 'platypus' – platypus being once common in the upper reaches. Maiwar proved elusive to the early European explorers, and it was not until a portion of ocean, discoloured by sediment, suggested the proximity of a major river system in the 18th century. This in turn provided an alert via an entry in a ship's log inviting closer scrutiny. Indeed, some historians believe that Portuguese seafarers had travelled down the each coast of the Australian continent in the 16th century.

This riparian paradise surrendered its anonymity in 1823 when three of four timber-getters, Thomas Pamphlett, John Finnegan and Richard Parsons (John Thompson having died at sea), stumbled upon an

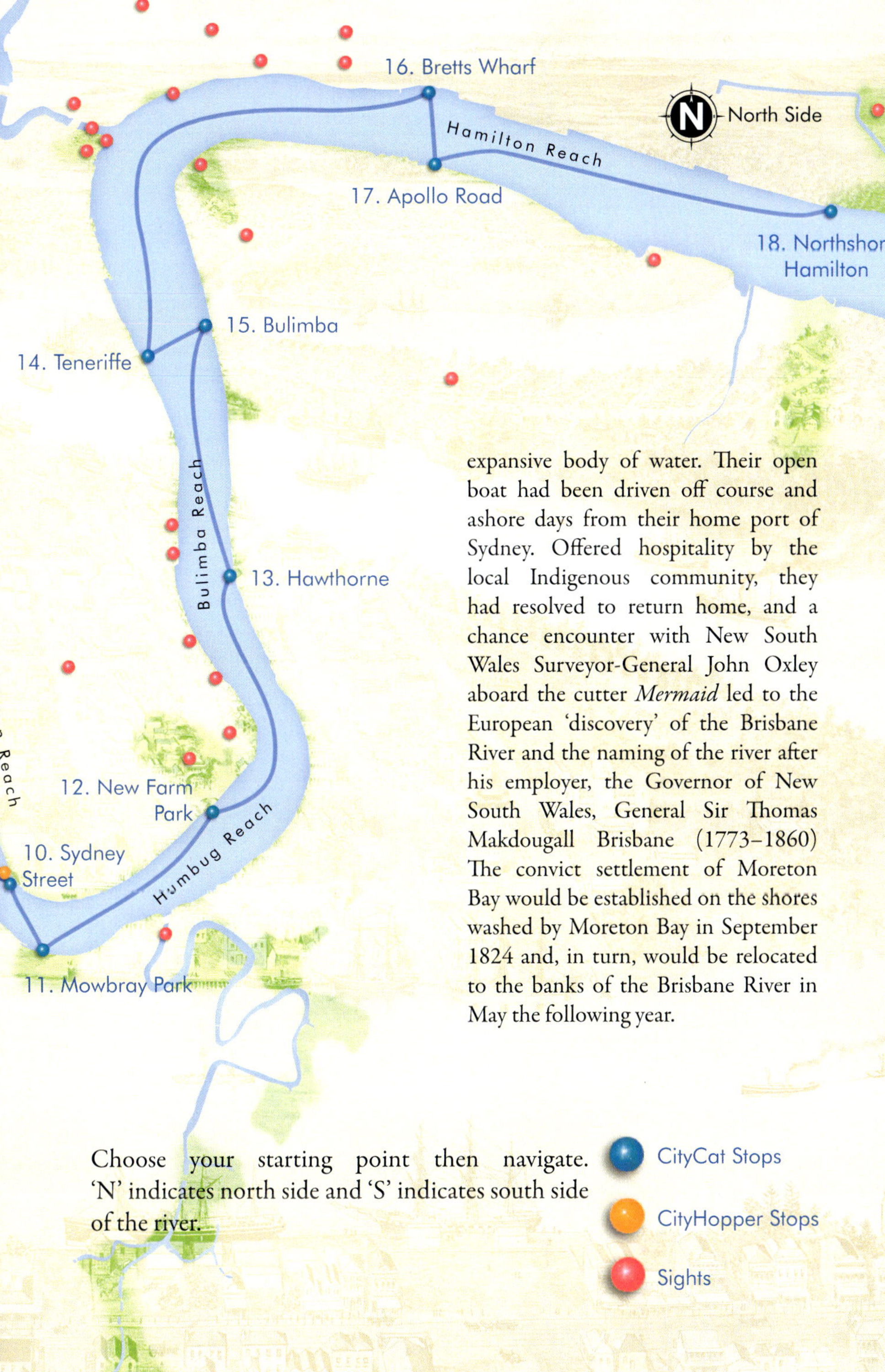

expansive body of water. Their open boat had been driven off course and ashore days from their home port of Sydney. Offered hospitality by the local Indigenous community, they had resolved to return home, and a chance encounter with New South Wales Surveyor-General John Oxley aboard the cutter *Mermaid* led to the European 'discovery' of the Brisbane River and the naming of the river after his employer, the Governor of New South Wales, General Sir Thomas Makdougall Brisbane (1773–1860) The convict settlement of Moreton Bay would be established on the shores washed by Moreton Bay in September 1824 and, in turn, would be relocated to the banks of the Brisbane River in May the following year.

Choose your starting point then navigate. 'N' indicates north side and 'S' indicates south side of the river.

The Brisbane River is the longest river in South East Queensland and flows through the city of Brisbane before emptying in Moreton Bay.

From its source around Mt Stanley, 344 kilometres to Moreton Bay, the Brisbane River, with its many twists and turns, presents the interested travelling public with a series of reaches with names that are at once geographic, historic and of social importance.

Significant floods have occurred several times since the European settlement of Brisbane. Seven major flood peaks have been recorded at the Brisbane gauge since records began in 1841, including:

14 January 1841, with a maximum river level of 8.43 metres at the gauge, the highest flood level recorded to date

1887, 1889, March 1890.

February 1893, a sequence of flood peaks (8.35 metres) over two weeks saw the highest recorded flood level in the Brisbane central business district. Seven lives were lost in the Eclipse Colliery at North Ipswich as a direct result of the flooding. Several other lives were lost to drownings.

March 1908, February 1931.

27 January 1974, the largest flood to affect Brisbane City in the 20th century, with a level of 5.45 metres.

11 January 2011, with a level of 4.46 metres.

28 January 2013 had a level of 2.3 metres.

St Lucia Reach

1. University of Queensland

The area of Long Pocket, St Lucia and western Toowong was all *'Tu-wong'* to Brisbane's First Nations. 'Tu-wong' was the plaintive call of the Rain Bird, an Asian species that nests here during the Rainy Season. It is said to call in the rains. The Rain Bird loved the area's rainforest fringes and many waterholes, which First Nations people used in rain-making ceremonies. Farming had begun at St Lucia in the 1850s and had morphed into the growing of sugar. The floating distillery *Walrus* was often to be seen in colonial times berthed alongside the riverbank not far from the UQ rowing sheds, with nearby Mill Road a 'signpost' to this earlier colourful history.

Travelling sugar-mill *Walrus* on the Albert River, c. 1870.
John Oxley Library

Ⓝ University of Queensland

St Lucia

The high parts of Dutton Park, like some rural dress circle, look down on this reach of the Brisbane River and across to the sprawling St Lucia campus of the University of Queensland. A new site for the university was made possible by a grant in 1927 by Dr James O'Neil Mayne and Mary Emelia Mayne of £50 000 to the Brisbane City Council to acquire 274 acres (111 ha) which, ultimately, enabled the university to move from its cramped operations at the bottom of George Street in a building that had formerly served as Government House.

From 1 August 1942 to 31 December 1944, when the campus was still being built, it became the site of the Advanced Land Headquarters (Adv LHQ) of the South-West Pacific Area theatre of war. General (later Field Marshall Sir) Thomas Blamey, who commanded all Allied land forces in the

Construction of the Forgan Smith Building, St Lucia, 1940.
John Oxley Library

SWPA, was based here. The bridge linking Dutton Park and St Lucia – opened in 2006 – goes under the names Green Bridge and the Eleanor Schonell and operates as a bridge for buses, cyclists and pedestrians. Its formal name is a nod to educationalist Eleanor Schonell (1902–1962), whose husband was University of Queensland Vice-Chancellor Sir Fred Schonell, who served in that capacity from 1960 to 1969.

2. West End

West End was a patch of rainforest known to First Nations people as *Kuril-pa*: 'Place of Bush Rats.' These were a native rat that lived in abundance in the vine forests. They were often corralled into this corner and netted in great numbers. This same corner – the end of this reach of the Brisbane River – is marked by the recreational reserve Orleigh Park at Hill End, reclaimed after the 1893 flood. From 1899 to 1906, Orleigh Park was 'Cranrook' – the home to which Aboriginal women and girls were forcibly removed, from all over Queensland, to be trained as domestic servants. A plaque and some steps mark this sad history.

Orleigh Park, West End

Up the hill on Dornoch Terrace is the iconic Torbrek residential unit block. Torbreck was completed in 1960 when Brisbane had no Building Ordinances for home units. Designed by architects Aubrey Job and Robert Froud, it became the first high-rise residential building in Brisbane. On the other side at Toowong lies Kayes Rocks. Named after Samuel Kaye, an appointment to the Toowong Shire Council, here was a most interesting man... a music teacher and member of the Toowong Philharmonic Orchestra who operated a museum for musical instruments.

Torbreck home units

House typically called a 'Queenslander'

3. Guyatt Park

What is now Guyatt Park was once a dense grove of hoop pine and unusual rainforest species that Oxley commented on and sampled, when exploring this area. A report in *The Sunday Mail* of 28 April 1929 provides this fascinating insight. Reporting on, among other prominent residents of the district, the newspaper talks of "Mr David Guyatt, whose old home and store is still standing in St Lucia Road".

More information is gleaned as the report continues, "Mr Guyatt's store, which in the early days served as the Post Office for the district, was originally situated on the lower flats, but the disastrous floods of 1893 were responsible for him moving the building to its present site on higher ground. A request to rename the Hiron Street Reserve as a tribute to the Guyatt Family in the early 1950s was proposed by the St Lucia Progress Association".

David Guyatt's store at the corner of Ryans Rd and Sir F Schonell Dr.
St Lucia History Group

Middenbury House (former ABC site)

Coronation Drive, Toowong

Built: 1865

From the former site of the Australian Broadcasting Corporation, the villa Middenbury watches over the river. This residence dates from 1865 when Mrs Eliza Rogers purchased six acres of land on which this residence was built.

Middenbury, a residence at Toowong, 1932.
John Oxley Library

Panoramic view of the South Brisbane Reach of the Brisbane River c. 1905.
John Oxley Library

Yachts in the Toowong Reach of the Brisbane River in front of the Regatta Hotel, 1897.
John Oxley Library

XXXX Brewery

Milton House

Cook Terrace

5. Milton

John Oxley Monument

Toowong Reach

Moorlands

Gas Stripping Tower

Regatta Hotel

4. Regatta Hotel

Middenbury House

Toowong, Milton, South Brisbane Reaches

ilton Reach

Foggitt, Jones & Co. Warehouse

Paul's Milk Factory

Victoria Bridge

Hector Vasyli Monument

6. North Quay

Treasury Building

Land Administration Building

Old Government Printing Offices

Commissariat Store

Old Immigration Depot

Parliament House

7. South Bank

8. QUT Gardens Point

North Quay and Milton Reach of the Brisbane River.
John Oxley Library

4. Regatta Hotel

Regatta Hotel

543 Coronation Drive, Toowong
Design: Richard Gailey
Built: 1886

The Regatta Hotel is strongly associated with the social and sporting life of the University of Queensland. In the 21st century, it is a multi-level hostelry, a far cry from the single-storey hotel of 1876 and just a cooee away from the Wesley Hospital. A covered stormwater outlet emptying into the river and a set of gardens just east of the hotel mark the remains of *Jo-ai Jo-ai* (literally 'fish') – the creek estuary and rocky platform that were once a favourite fishing spot for First Nations people and settlers. A newsletter article dated 19 March 1887 speaks in glowing terms of this new hostelry:

Floodwaters around the Regatta Hotel, March 1908.
John Oxley Library

This splendid hotel has been opened by its enterprising proprietor Mr Wenterford. Probably, not even in Brisbane, is there another hotel to which in appearance the Regatta Hotel would stand second. Certainly, there was no hotel in Queensland that has a finer situation.

Over three floors, the building boasted a dining room capable of seating up to 100, billiard room, private sitting rooms, bedrooms, hot and cold water and gas throughout.

In the 1893 and 1974 floods, the water came to the first floor.

Moorlands

451 Coronation Drive, Auchenflower

Design: Richard Gailey
Built: 1892

Moorlands had replaced an earlier property known as Moorlands Villa. Moorlands will be forever linked to the Mayne family (who owned it until 1940). The estate was purchased in 1971 for the development of the Wesley Hospital. The area was once a large base camp and corroboree ground. Oxley made some of his first contacts with First Nations' people here.

Moorlands residence at Toowong, c. 1918.
John Oxley Library

Gas Stripping Tower

277 Montague Road, West End

The question is begged... what about the lighthouse? While it might have the height and bearing, it is, in fact, a gas stripping tower, an important part of Brisbane's industrial history dating from 1912 when it was brought in pieces from Robert Hempster & Son, Yorkshire and saw service at the South Brisbane Gas & Light Company's works at Montague Road through until the 1970s and then, in 1988, was relocated to its present site.

John Oxley Monument

Coronation Drive, Milton

Built: 1988

One of Brisbane's oldest formal memorials may not even be an appropriate memorial if one is to believe more recent research. An early memorial to NSW Surveyor-General John Oxley is located on the ridge now called North Quay. Its inspiration was born out of the 1925 Centenary Celebrations and indeed a surplus of £2500 following said celebrations provided the necessary funding for this memorial, with a plaque alluding to the argument that here was the place that Oxley stopped in search of water. In the light of subsequent research, it begs the question... was John Oxley a mountain goat?' such is the climb up from the river bank.

John Oxley would make three journeys up the river, which he named after his employer who lived at Parramatta in the colony of New South Wales...

John Oxley Monument,North Quay, c. 1932.

John Oxley Library

December 1823, September 1824 and November 1824. Indeed a second John Oxley Memorial is not far away, on a bank overlooking the Milton Reach of the Brisbane River; a 'chain of ponds' that was a highlight in earlier times of parts of the present-day suburbs of Milton and Auchenflower and that may just be where John Oxley really did stop in search of water!

John Oxley Monument, Milton

Milton Reach

5. Milton

Cook Terrace

249 Coronation Drive, Milton

Builder: Joseph Blain Cook
Built: 1888

Subsidence along the River Road, Coronation Drive, c. 1893.
John Oxley Library

These two-storey brick structures, known collectively as Cook Terrace after builder Joseph Blain Cook, dated from the 1880s, a period in Brisbane's architectural time of Belle Epoch proportions.

This rare example of a Victorian streetscape also marks the entrance to Milton's Park Avenue, which offers many shopping experiences and even boasts a miniature Eiffel Tower.

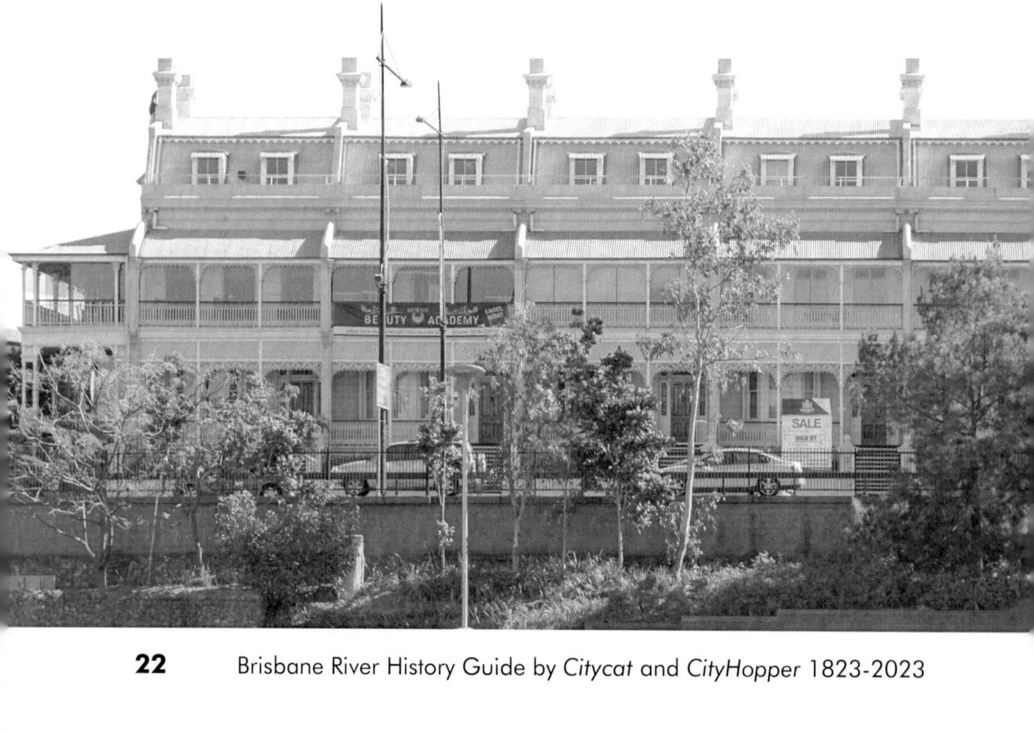

Milton House

50 McDougall Street, Milton
Built: 1852 to 1922

Members of the Manning family on the side veranda of Milton House, c. 1870.
John Oxley Library

From its lofty shoreline position, Milton House joins other residences that look down upon a reach long identified with sailing and rowing regattas like 'The Head of the River' and a significant stand of *Araucaria cunninghamii*; hoop pine – which Surveyor-General Oxley saw as having the potential to be used as masts and spars for sailing ships. A patch of rainforest terminated just below the house – marked by a First Nations' camp and dance ground.

XXXX Brewery

185 Milton Rd, Milton

Founded: 1878

Castlemaine Perkins staff outside the brewery in Milton, c. 1929.
John Oxley Library

At night as clouds of steam compete with the disarming red glow of four neon Xs (1959) and the smell of hops permeates the air, it looks anything but a brewery manufacturing a bitter ale for which it has become famous. There has been a brewery on this site since 1878... the creation of a partnership bringing together the Fitzgerald family of the Castlemaine Brewery at Castlemaine in Victoria and the Quinlans, who manufactured rum a short distance away from the current site.

The 'Perkins' part of the business is linked to Toowoomba brewer, businessman and, ultimately, politician Patrick Perkins (1838-1901), who entered the beer business in Brisbane and by 1928, following restructuring, the brand Castlemaine Perkins name came into existence.

Foggitt, Jones & Co. Warehouse

Sandwiched between the Merivale and Go Between bridges is a remnant of early Brisbane industry, the one-time warehouse/factory of Foggitt & Jones, manufacturer of camp pie and turtle soup and other culinary 'delights'.

Adjacent is Paul's Milk Factory, now Parmalat, a history that commenced with the opening of the factory on the banks of the Brisbane River back in the 1930s.

NOT MOCK Turtle Soup, but Pure Essence of Fresh Meat of REAL TURTLE from the Barrier Reef....

REX real Turtle Soup

Perhaps the most Nutritious Food there is.

FOGGITT, JONES PTY., LTD.

Bridges

Approaching the end of the Milton Reach, the viewer is confronted by a quartet of bridges... the Go Between, the William Jolly, Merivale Cross-River Rail Link and Kurilpa pedestrian bridge.

The Grey Street Bridge (known as the William Jolly from 1955) cost £384 850 and drew as its inspiration a rainbow arch bridge from St Paul in Minnesota in the United States. The year of its official opening – 1932 – was also the year when the Sydney Harbour Bridge opened for business.

Originally part of a broader scheme for the construction of 11 bridges to cross the Brisbane River to ease traffic congestion, the dream is unrealised. The Merivale Cross-River Rail Link built in November 1978 is a nod to the rainbow arches of the nearby William Jolly Bridge, while the Kurilpa pedestrian bridge (seen with affection by some as the Fiddle-Sticks Bridge) acknowledges the Indigenous name meaning 'place of the bush rat'. This was a major First Nations' crossing point for canoes and people – sometimes

Kurilpa pedestrian bridge

swimming over in groups of 50 to 60. It once sported a sandy beach and occasional camps. The Go Between, finished in July 2010, acknowledges the 1977 indie rock band formed in Brisbane and its music, most notably *Streets of our Town* from 1988.

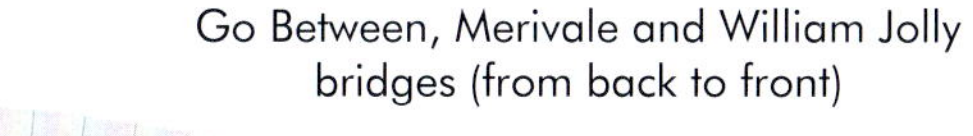

Go Between, Merivale and William Jolly bridges (from back to front)

Cultural Precinct

The Queensland Cultural Centre looms large. The area was originally the core of South Brisbane – a rather 'Wild West' assortment of hotels and docks where much of the wool and beef from the Logan and Darling Downs were shipped off in the 1840s-1860s. Many First Nations people worked on the Docks or sold honey and fish at the former wharves. This association may explain why this area became the 'Coloured Zone' during World War 2. During the 1940s-1950s, it had many hostels and clubs for Black Americans and Aboriginal people. With a majority of the Centre – The Queensland Performing Arts Centre, State Library of Queensland, Queensland Art Gallery and Queensland Museum – designed by Robin Gibson & Partners in 1985, it was subsequently joined by the Kerry & Lindsay Clare-designed Gallery of Modern Art, which opened in December 2006. The Precinct was Heritage-listed in June 2015.

Victoria Bridge

Design: Coordinator-General's Department
Built: 1969

The Victoria Bridge of today is, ostensibly, the third permanent bridge, with previous bridges constructed using a variety of materials in 1865, 1874 (a portion of which was washed away in the floods of 1893), 1897 and today's bridge, dating from 1969.

First permanent Victoria Bridge, 1874.
John Oxley Library

Victoria Bridge

Second permanent Victoria Bridge, 1906.
John Oxley Library

Hector Vasyli Memorial

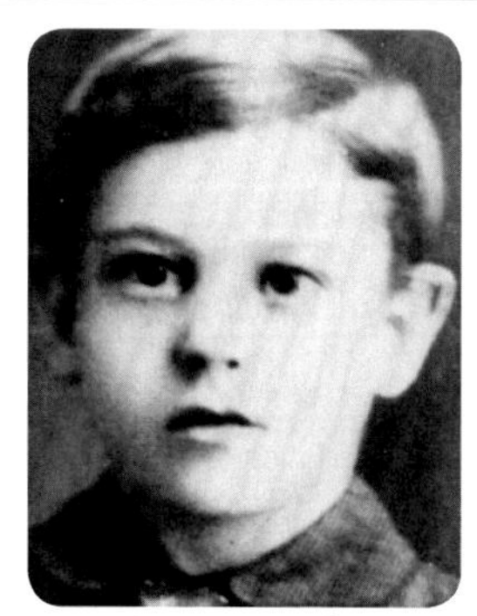

Hector Vasyli.
John Oxley Library

A memorial to the Australian-Greek paperboy Hector Vasyli, killed while welcoming home World War I veterans, is placed on part of the south-side presidium to the 1897 bridge.

Remnant of the second Victoria Bridge

Hector Vasyli plaque, 1918.
John Oxley Library

6. North Quay

North Quay – also called Queens Wharf – is a heritage precinct that saw the earliest (convict period) European occupation of Brisbane. It was originally a ridge of blue gum forest with occasional First Nations' camps.

Treasury Building

130 William St, Brisbane.

Design: John James Clark
Built: 1889, 1893, 1928

On the CBD side of the Victoria Bridge is the Treasury Casino, which operates out of the shell of the Renaissance-inspired Treasury Building, the first section of which dates from 1885, Brisbane's Belle Epoch in terms of significant architectural treasures. Built on the site of the Officers' Quarters and Military Barracks of convict times to a

Treasury Building, Brisbane, 1896.
John Oxley Library

design of Queensland's Colonial Architect John James Clark, this was a building built over three stages and forty years. The last stage, the facade on George and Queen streets, was finished in 1928. In its new guise as a casino, this building reopened in April 1995.

Former State Library

Cnr. William Street and Elizabeth Street, Brisbane.

Design: FDG Stanley
Built: 1879

Beyond the Riverside Expressway, the former State Library of Queensland comes into view; its Leonard Shillam installation entitled *Enlightenment* reinforcing the fact that, even earlier in 1879, this purpose-built building was the Queensland Museum. In 1896 the Brisbane Public Library was established in William Street and on 29 April 1902 this building was recycled as the Public Library of Queensland, the Museum having moved to the Exhibition building.

Old Queensland Museum, Brisbane, c. 1885.
John Oxley Library

Land Administration Building

142 George Street, Brisbane.

Design: Thomas Pye
Built: 1905

Directly across the road from this building the Treasury Hotel, formerly the Executive Building, was constructed from 1901 to 1905. The construction cost £14 000. It has served many masters, including the home of the Queensland National Art Gallery until 1930 and overlooks, among other memorials, the one and only statue of Queen Victoria, who gave Queensland its name.

Executive Building, Brisbane, c. 1907.
John Oxley Library

Land Administration Building

Commissariat Store

115 William St, Brisbane.

Built: 1829 extended 1913

Commissariat Store extension 1913.
Queensland State Archives

The three-storey Commissariat Store is a neighbour, separated by a verdant space known by the name Miller Park, named for the founding Commandant of the Convict Settlement of Moreton Bay, Lieutenant Henry Miller (1809-1888). The Store – now HQ of the Royal Historical Society of Queensland – dates from 1829, a rare relic of Brisbane's convict legacy. As the Commissariat Store it had a major role, providing the fledgling convict settlement on the banks of the Brisbane River with the produce, cloths and tools to operate. A regular ferry that ran between here and South Brisbane was originally the main crossing between the two sides of Brisbane. The boatmen were often First Nations people from Stradbroke Island. Its top floor, which looks just so right in proportion to the rest of the building, was added in 1913.

Old Immigration Depot

99 William Street

Design: Charles Tiffin
Built: 1865-1899

It is home to a number of organisations, with the preservation of Brisbane's history front and centre; a far cry from its original role as an Immigration Depot dating from 1865 to 1866.

Old Government Printing Offices

110 George Street

Design: Francis Drummond Greville Stanley, Edwin Evan Smith
Built: 1874, 1887, 1912

The former Government Printing Office, recognised by a steeply pitched roof, occupied the site of an earlier Government Printing Office. This was the first element of a complex that extended through to George Street and was another example of the work of architect FDG Stanley.

Government first printing office, c. 1869.
John Oxley Library

7. South Bank

SouthBank

South Bank was originally part of Kurilpa rainforest – a jungle of palms, tree ferns, orchids and staghorns. From 1827 to 1830, after being cleared and planted with corn, the area was scene to bloody skirmishes, as groups of 50-80 First Nations warriors continually raided and destroyed the corn, in an effort to starve out the penal colony. After this (in the 1840s), the abandoned fields were turned into paddocks for the horses of the Border Police, who were ancestral to the dreaded Native Mounted Police. South Bank also saw a battle in 1850 between Chinese immigrants and local Aboriginal people.

Today South Bank Parklands is very much marketed as a pleasure palace of the 21st century; a far cry from its earlier roles as a busy commercial district complete with iconic flour mill and hotels and its rejuvenation as the site of EXPO 88 (April–October 1988). Several sites, reflective of those earlier times, survive.

The South Brisbane Dry Dock (see Maritime Museum) welcomed its first customer in September 1881. Nearby is the Ship Inn, a hotel of many names and reputations down through the years with, 10 June 1879 the first recorded use of the name 'Ship Inn'. With significant social changes that began with the construction of the Story Bridge and the limitations to overseas shipping that resulted; the closure of the coaling wharf spur line and, ultimately, the discontinuation of trams along Stanley Street, it was, for a time, a struggle for this hotel to survive.

The Plough Inn dating from 1885 was a creation of South Brisbane's commercial fortunes at that time; a most elaborate hotel standing on the site of an earlier hotel and the pride and joy of publican Daniel Costigan. The Plough Inn of colonial times (of which a good part of the exterior survives) was built at a cost of £3000 to a design by Alexander Wilson and built by Abraham Jones.

The third listed site celebrates the role of EXPO 88 in breathing new life into a precinct rich in the Indigenous and European historical narrative. The EXPO 88 Nepalese Peace Pagoda of three levels is but one of three outside the Nation of Nepal; the product of 160 Kathmandu Valley craftsmen that was brought to Brisbane and assembled; albeit on another site within the EXPO precinct.

Watson Ferguson printers offices before demolition, 1983.
John Oxley Library

8. QUT, Gardens Point

Parliament House

Gardens Point, Brisbane
Design: Charles Tiffin
Built: 1865-1867, 1878, 1887, 1889

Parliament House, c. 1869.
John Oxley Library

Work on the historic Parliament House in George Street commenced in 1864 with occupation four years later and, following further extensions, was finally completed in 1889.

Looking more at home in the countryside of the Loire Valley in France, this grandly proportioned building was built to the design of Charles Tiffin (1833-1873).

Maritime Museum

South Bank

Dry dock: 1870s
Founded: 1971

The Queensland Maritime Museum is built in and around the former South Brisbane Dry Dock, a by-product of a time when the South Brisbane Reach of the Brisbane River welcomed ships from around the world. Parts of the little inlet are natural. It was once a cove of vine forest with figs and yellow wood, where the waterholes of Woolloongabba occasionally tipped into the river via a waterfall. Beside this was a winter camp that First Nations' people used, as the area was protected from the wind. The barque *Doon* christened the dry dock in 1881, a long time since 1876 when work of the site commenced. Acknowledged as the third oldest dry dock in Australia – and pre-dated by the Fitzroy Dry Dock in Sydney

Two boats using the graving docks at South Brisbane, c. 1910.
John Oxley Library

[1847] and Alfred Graving Dock at Williamstown, Victoria [1864]) –the South Brisbane Dry Dock was at its busiest in the years before The Great War.

Today the museum is home to all manner of nauticalia, in particular the RAN 'River Class' frigate *Diamantina* and steam tug *Forceful*. The Diamantina carried Japanese officers to two of the main Japanese surrenders that marked the end of World War II. Its quarterdeck was used for the signings of one of these.

Maritime Museum with South Brisbane Town Hall in the background

South Brisbane Town Hall

263 Vulture Street
Design: John S Murdock
Built: 1891

South Brisbane Town Hall c. 1892.
John Oxley Library

The old South Brisbane Town Hall is a building complete with tower that signified an oh-so-subtle battle between the north and south sides of a community freed of its shackles as a convict settlement.

Commissioned for the South Brisbane Municipal Council, the building was constructed between 1891 and 1892 to a design attributed to John S Murdock who would later serve as Chief Architect of the Commonwealth. The cost initially was to be £6999, however, the final cost blew up to £11 000. Post the introduction of 'Greater Brisbane', this building has fulfilled many roles... flats for Council employees, service to both the Australian Army and the American Military Police and home to the Conservatorium of Music.

Birds

Under Captain Cook Bridge are plugs that are remnants of the old coaling wharves. Look carefully, for you just might see an ancient bird sitting atop said plugs!

All Hallows
Howard Smith Wharves
Story Bridge
Petrie Bight Wall
Customs House
Captain Burke Park
Jazz Club
9. Riverside
Holman St
Yungaba
Shafston Reach
Naval Stores
St Mary the Virgin
Queensland Polo Club
Naval Offices
Dockside
Graving Docks
Town Reach
Thornton St
10. Sydney St
Parliament House
Botanic Gardens
Shafston House
8. QUT Gardens Point
South Brisbane Reach
Kangaroo Point Cliffs
Birds
Lamb House
Maritime Museum

Town and Shafston Reaches

This part of the river is among the busiest and most historically crowded with bridges embracing the reach... the Story Bridge, named for public servant and University of Queensland Vice-Chancellor JD Story, and the Captain Cook Bridge, a cross-river extension to the Riverside Expressway.

It was once a busy reach of the river, a riverside, or near riverside home at various times, to the Customs House, assorted shipping agencies, marine insurance underwriters, the Port Office, Water Police and market.

A part of the river that saw Queensland's greatest peacetime maritime tragedy in February 1896 when the ferry *Pearl* came in contact with the anchor chain of the Queensland Government yacht *Lucinda* during a time when the Brisbane River was in flood, resulting in the capsizing of the ferry.

Ships moored at Circular Quay in the Brisbane River, 1884.

All Hallows' School can be seen high on the hill to the left. The photograph is looking from Kangaroo Point across the river towards Fortitude Valley and New Farm.

John Oxley Library

Lamb House

9 Leopard Street, Kangaroo Point
Design: Alexander Brown Wilson
Built: 1902-1908

Lamb House, Kangaroo Point, c. 1904.
John Oxley Library

With spectacular vistas across Brisbane to the foothills of Mt Coot-tha, this imposing mansion simply called Home was constructed by W Anthony. It was built for John Lamb of the drapery company Edwards & Lamb at a cost of £3250. Its many levels embody the essence of a residence built in the Federation architectural style. The area along the river terrace just below Lamb House was once a thicket of wattle and she-oak that served as a funerary area for First Nations people. The deceased – often from the nearby camps and tournament grounds at Woolloongabba – were interred on platforms here.

Botanic Gardens

147 Alice St, Brisbane City

Design: Walter Hill
Founded: 1855

Brisbane's Botanic Gardens from Parliament House, c. 1889.
John Oxley Library

This verdant refuge from the adjacent busy Brisbane commercial business district was much smaller in 1828 when New South Wales Colonial Botanist Charles Fraser surveyed the area as a public garden for the convict settlement. It was called *Binbilla* by First Nations' people. It was an area of rainforest, swamps, and ponds. Originally, it had many groves of tulipwood, which were used to make spears. *Meanjin* – 'like a spike of a spear' – the name for Brisbane CBD – probably derived from the use of these groves and from the shape of the CBD area.

The gardens are now almost 200 years old – some of the oldest in Australia. They were expanded to an area of 50 acres through the amalgamation of surrounding reserves. It was sometimes a zoo and during the floods of 1893, a repository of ships washed ashore. The horticulturalist Walter Hill (1819–1904) harvested and experimented with plantings from around the world and the avenue of *Araucaria bidwillii* was planted by Hill in honour of JC Bidwill. Many of Queensland's crops were first trialled here, and many of the state's bush tucker plants were first grown and promoted here by Walter Hill.

Kangaroo Point Cliffs

The Triassic-period volcanic tuff here and similar cliffs at Petrie's Bight and under the William Jolly Bridge were viewed by First Nations people as walls raised by the slithering of the gigantic Dreaming Serpent/Eel as she gouged out the river valley. Today abseilers nimbly navigate these cliffs, which represent a significant part of Brisbane's cityscape. From 1826 until 1976 this was a quarry producing Brisbane Tuff for various projects in South-East Queensland including many colonial buildings of the CBD. Floodlit at night, this part of the City attracted the attention of New South Wales Surveyor-General John Oxley who, in giving the river its name Brisbane in December 1823, referred to the area as a 'high, rocky bank'.

St Mary the Virgin Church

455 Main St, Kangaroo Point

Design: Richard G Suter
Built: 1873-1931

There has been a St Mary's Church at Kangaroo Point since 1849 and this church is recognised as ministering to Brisbane's naval community beginning with the Queensland Marine Defence Force and, more recently, the Royal Australian Navy. The church of 1873 was modified following damage caused by a cyclone in 1893 and today houses the Voyager Memorial, commemorating the loss of the Daring-class destroyer HMAS *Voyager* following a collision between this ship and the RAN Flagship HMAS *Melbourne* in February 1964 in which the *Voyager* was sunk.

St Mary's Anglican Church at Kangaroo Point, 1892.
John Oxley Library

Naval Stores

34 Amesbury Street, Kangaroo Point

Built: 1886-1900s

Nestled at the base of the cliffs of Kangaroo Point is evidence of the Naval Stores that serviced Queensland's colonial navy from the arrival in Brisbane of the first gunboats *Gayundah* (1884) and *Paluma* (1885). It was not all smooth sailing for this Queensland Marine Defence Force, which grew in the number of ships and the size of its collective ships company' and it was not without scandal and misadventure; at one stage a mutiny of sorts being contemplated in 1888.

Naval Stores at Kangaroo Point seen from across the Brisbane River.
John Oxley Library

Naval Offices

3 Edward Street, Brisbane
Built: 1900-1901

This area and the nearby Eagle Street Pier were the original 'entry point' for foreign dignitaries and royalty visiting Brisbane in the colonial era. Consequently, there were many processions from this point into Brisbane during the 1860s-1900s. Sometimes parties of Aboriginal warriors met these visitors here and paraded along the streets as part of an official welcome.

With its pediment conveniently hinting at its year of construction and a nautical logo confirming its role as Naval Offices at the time of Federation, this is one of Brisbane's most significant buildings and was indicative of the growing influence of the new State of Queensland which, interestingly, had not generally favoured the federation of the Australian Colonies into the new Nation of Australia in 1901. This was despite the efforts of Federation advocates like Sir Samuel Griffith, Sir Robert Dickson and JM Macrossan.

With its tuck-pointed face brickwork and decorative chimneys among other decorative elements, the building evokes a Queen Ann revivalist style that complements its neighbour, the facade of the FDG Stanley-designed Port Office of earlier times.

Commandant of the Queensland Marine Defence Force at this auspicious time of Federation was William Rooke Creswell, a fervent advocate for the creation of a stand-alone Australian Navy. Indeed Creswell, came to be known as The Father of the Royal Australian Navy.

Naval Offices in Edward Street, c. 1901.
John Oxley Library

Brisbane Polo Club (Naldham House)

190 Mary St, Brisbane
Built: 1864 and 1889

Naldham House, premises of the Australian United Steam Navigation Company, Mary Street.
John Oxley Library

Ocean-going ships are nowhere to be seen in the Town Reach of today, yet a cupola overlooking the Brisbane River demands further attention, a building in the High Victorian tradition that would seem more at home in the docklands of Mumbai.

The building is best remembered as Naldham House; Naldham, a subset of Macdonald Hamilton, agents for the iconic shipping company AUSN. It was placed on the Queensland Heritage Register in 1992. In its present form, Naldham House, sans the warehouse that once augmented the precinct, dates from 1889 although, with the ships long gone, new businesses occupy its floors.

Customs House

399 Queen St, Brisbane
Design: Charles McLay
Built: 1886 to 1889

Old Customs House, c. 1889.
John Oxley Library

Best viewed from the Brisbane River, the Customs House's exuberant architecture reflects the commercial prosperity of the 1880s. To a design prepared by Charles McLay and constructed by the well-known builder John Petrie & Son, the Customs House opened for business on 2 September 1889; replacing an earlier structure that had been constructed after Moreton Bay had been declared a Port of Entry in 1846.

Ⓝ Petrie Bight Wall

The cliffs here mark another 'bend' of the Dreaming Serpent's meanderings. The area above the cliff was used as a dance ground by First Nations' people. The unique wall seen from the Brisbane River is Heritage-listed and dates from 1881-82 when it was constructed by the Brisbane Municipal Council at a cost of £7000. This cost allowed for the construction of the wall and the extension to the Kennedy Wharf at Petrie Bight; the name 'Petrie' referring to the nearby home of a significant Brisbane family who first had links with the convict settlement of Moreton Bay.

Ⓢ Jazz Club

1 Annie Street, Kangaroo Point

It was built as a boat club in the 1930s. On 15 April 1972, two members of the Adventurers Club rowed Lord Mayor Clem Jones across the Brisbane River in a canoe for the opening ceremony.

All Hallows'

547 Ann Street, Brisbane

Design: Andrea Stombuco
Built: 1882

Recognised as the first permanent site of the Convent and School of the Sisters of Mercy in Queensland, All Hallows – thought to have been named by Mother Vincent Whitty – grew up around the home of Dr George Fullerton, which was acquired for £6000. In the years that followed a number of extensions were added, notably those of Italian-born Andrea Stombuco.

All Hallows' convent, 1889.
John Oxley Library

Shafston Reach

Story Bridge

Design: John Bradfield
Built: 1935 to 1939

Story Bridge in the fourth stage of construction, 1938.
John Oxley Library

A defining symbol of the City of Brisbane, the Story Bridge marks another major First Nations' crossing point – one associated with frequent bull shark attacks. The construction was the result of considerable agitation for another bridge across the Brisbane River. Work on this steel cantilever bridge,

Story Bridge with remnants of Evans Deakin shipyard at forefront.

inspired by the Jacques Cartier Bridge in Montreal, commenced in May 1935 and the north side and south side spans were joined in October 1939. Costing £1.6 million, this bridge, originally proposed to be called the Jubilee, opened in 1940 and operated as a toll bridge until 1947.

Ⓢ Captain John Burke Park

117 Holman Street

This park under the Story Bridge was originally a natural corral into which First Nations people regularly drove kangaroos. This – and the peninsula's resemblance to a kangaroo tail – is why it was known as *Maree* (or *Mari*) to the First Australians – their word for an adult male kangaroo. It is now 'Kangaroo Point', with the park becoming a funky maritime-inspired play space, and the scene to many concerts and picnics. The park's name acknowledges a ship-owning family of John Burkes whose ships, with their distinctive green, black and white funnels, traded along the Queensland coast as far as Torres Strait.

Yungaba

25 Anderson St, Kangaroo Point

Design: William Peter Clark
Built: 1887

Yungaba Immigration Depot at Kangaroo Point, 1907.
John Oxley Library

In the shadow of the Story Bridge mature trees hint at the existence of a substantial example of Brisbane's built environment, the purpose-built Kangaroo Point Immigration Depot, which welcomed its first immigrants in 1888.

In the years that followed this Depot hosted many a new arrival to Queensland and, in response to the challenges of the time, responded to other requests... as a reception centre for troops returning from the South African War, as a hospital and as an office during the time that the Story Bridge was being constructed.

Graving Docks

26 Cairns St, Kangaroo Point

Evans Deakin Shipyards at Kangaroo Point, 1963.
John Oxley Library

One-time graving dock (Peter's Slip) and shipyard and fitting-out wharf (Evans Deakin). Indeed the suburb of Kangaroo Point has had a number of renewals over its history.

Shafston House

46 Thorn St, Kangaroo Point

Design: Robin Dods
Built: 1851 to 1930s

Front of the residence Shafston built on the site of the original Shafston House, 1930.
John Oxley Library

The mansion Shafston was home to Henry Stuart Russell, who wrote *The Genesis of Queensland*. Subsequently, it was an ANZAC Hostel, HQ of a kindergarten organisation, private residence and an educational institution.

10. Sydney Street

CityHopper

Directly across from Evans Deakin was the wharf for the Commonwealth Lighthouse Service, and over the years ships servicing lighthouses along the Queensland coast have included *Cape Leeuwin*, *Cape Moreton* and *Cape Don*. Today this precinct in the suburb of New Farm has been redeveloped as a riverside apartment complex and is one of the points of entry for the much-loved riverside walk that has been reconstructed after earlier floods tore away an earlier structure.

There is an example of a lightship in the Queensland Maritime Museum.

Lighthouse servicer *Carpentaria*, 1919.

John Oxley Library

The *Carpentaria*, one of several vessels built for the Commonwealth Lighthouse Service. They are crewless, light being supplied during hours of darkness by means of a special automatic apparatus. Each boat carries enough compressed gas to last for a year. The *Carpentaria* was lying at one of Brisbane's wharves last week en route for the Gulf of Carpentaria, where she will be stationed.

The Queenslander, supplement, 31 May 1919

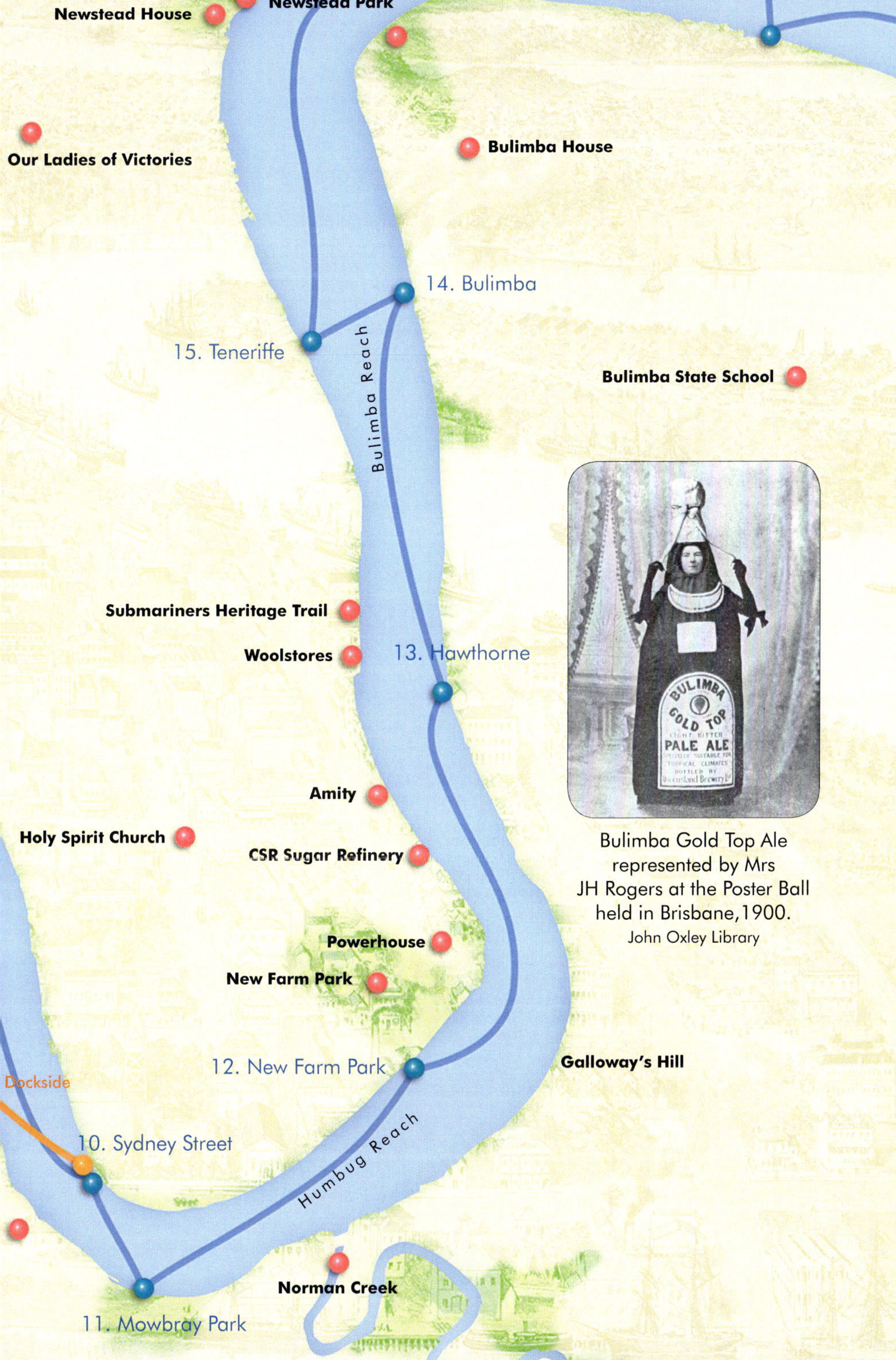

Bulimba Gold Top Ale represented by Mrs JH Rogers at the Poster Ball held in Brisbane, 1900.
John Oxley Library

Humbug and Bulimba Reaches

The origins of Humbug Reach appear anecdotal, with one suggestion being that sailing vessels making their way up the Brisbane River would often become becalmed in this reach because the cliffs of Galloway's Hill acted as a natural barrier, prompting an oath from those aboard the ill-starred vessel.

Originally given the compliment of 'The Noble Reach' by botanist and explorer Allan Cunningham in 1824, the subsequent name Bulimba Reach came about due to a brewery that had opened in Oxford Street in 1882. Having failed within the year, its operations were acquired by the Queensland Brewery Company, and this Company's larger site dating from 1906 saw a move to the other side of the river.

Postcard of two steamships in the Brisbane River at Bulimba, looking south, c. 1907.
John Oxley Library

11. Mowbray Park

Mowbray Park

Lytton Road, East Brisbane
Founded: 1904

The area between Mowbray Park and Shaftson House was the site of a traditional Aboriginal camp and tournament (fighting) ground, which were still in use into the 1870s. Regularly at dusk, police would drive Aboriginal people out of the 'town boundaries' (in this case, Wellington Road) and into the park.

The whole suburb was formerly known as Mowbraytown; hence Mowbray Park and Mowbray Terrace. The name came from the Rev. Thomas Mowbray. Riversdale, the estate, was sold in 1903 to the South Brisbane Council for £6000, the Council having decided that it would become a public park. The old house on the site was sold for removal for £9 in the same year. Sadly, no photographs have ever been found of the old house (Riversdale). Mowbray Park is home to the City's oldest War Memorial to the men and women of World War I. It was often the venue for fetes to fund-raise for the war wounded. Adjacent to the ferry terminal is the site of an enclosed riverside swimming baths.

Mowbray Park on the banks of the Brisbane River, c. 1910.
John Oxley Library

Norman Creek

Norman Creek is a small tributary of the Brisbane River. It was formerly a rainforest pocket noted for its native limes, figs and lilly-illy berries. The spot had Aboriginal camps and an important fishing complex. This was one of the main areas from which First Nations people supplied fish, possum pelts and honey to Brisbane and South Brisbane.

It is serviced by the Canning Bridge, the most recent of several bridges since the area was developed. Over the years it acquired two names... Norman's Creek and Gorman Creek. Which one was correct?

Land sales are recorded as occurring from 1858 and the first recorded bridge over the mouth of the creek dated from 1856. Over the years Churchie rowing sculls and whaleboats belong to TS Magnus were often seen.

Peaceful scene at Norman Creek, Brisbane, 1889.
John Oxley Library

12. New Farm Park

New Farm Park

New Farm

Founded: 1914

New Farm Park, 1937.
John Oxley Library

The suburb of New Farm that meant, literally, the new farm that suppled the convict settlement of Moreton Bay. The area was originally wetlands: extensive, open marshes, lagoons and some paperbark swamps. It was one of the most important hunting grounds of the Brisbane First Nations, as it had many eels, snakes, water birds, *bungwall* fern (an edible tuber) and – most of all – barbel freshwater tortoises, which were caught in nets or by hand. It was called *Binkin-pa* ('place of the tortoise') for this reason.

This was a place of horse-racing in the 1840s, and has become one of the most celebrated garden parks of Brisbane.

New Farm Park bandstand.
John Oxley Library

Powerhouse

119 Lamington St, New Farm
Design: Roy Rusden Ogg
Built: 1927-1940

The recycled Powerhouse – now a place of artistic and theatrical endeavour – served the people of Brisbane from 1927 until 1971 and, at one stage, provided all the power for the City's fleet of trams.

Tramway Power House, New Farm, 1929.
John Oxley Library

CSR Sugar Refinery

Lamington Street, New Farm
Built: 1892

While the name 'Cutter's Landing' may be a commercial confection (and a nod to the cane-cutters whose endeavours contributed much to the prosperity of the Colonial Sugar Refinery), the Refinery is all that survives of a enclave of significant heritage-listed sites, and that has been reborn as much sought-after apartments.

Colonial Sugar Refinery, New Farm, c. 1902.
John Oxley Library

Following experiments with the growing of sugar by John Buhot and Louis Hope, plantations were established close to Brisbane and beyond, and by 1874 the colony of Queensland was exporting sugar to other Australian colonies. This industry was long a barometer of Queensland's economic prosperity; an industry acknowledged in the Coat of Arms of Queensland accorded the Colony in 1893.

Amity House

101 Welsby Street, New Farm
Built: 1892-1900s

Reflecting his love of all matters riparian, Amity was constructed for Thomas Welsby (1858-1941), an accountant, businessman. politician, athlete and author who wrote extensively on many matters pertaining to Moreton Bay. In later years when the Naval Depot HMAS *Moreton* was a neighbour, the residence was home to the Naval Officer commanding Queensland.

Holy Spirit Catholic Church

16 Villers St, New Farm
Design: Jack Donoghue
Built: 1927-30

"The present church, was an architectural gem, on a very fine central site... The design of the new church, said Archbishop Duhig, pleased him very much: in many respects, and particularly in the facade, the church was a welcome departure from other classes of ecclesiastical architecture in this country, no matter how commendable they might be. The beauty was enhanced by the use of Benedict stone, the texture of which was admirable, and which was crowned by the fine sculptural group which filled the tympanum."

The Brisbane Courier, 2 June 1930

13. Hawthorne

Hawthorne Ferry Terminal

Scott and Lindsay Streets

Built: 1925

Built shortly after the more prominent Bulimba terminal, they were at the time the largest and most ornamental terminals built in that era.

Woolstores

53 Vernon Terrace

Built: 1909, 1915, 1950s
Mactaggart's Woolstore was built in 1926

Woolstore building, Teneriffe, Brisbane, 1928.
John Oxley Library

With the sale overseas of bales of wool an integral part of Australia's economy, many of these wool stores are heritage-listed and in the 21st century have been transformed into loft apartments.

This was the reach of the river that once welcomed ships belonging to the British-registered Shaw Savill, Alfred Holt, the China Navigation Company and, in later years, the Dutch-registered Royal Interocean Line.

Submariners Walk Heritage Trail

Teneriffe

In World War II, many an Allied submarine was repaired at HMAS *Moreton* and elsewhere in this reach. On the opposite bank below Lourdes Hill College decompression trials of submariners took place.

HMAS *Moreton* site, New Farm, 1998.
Brisbane City Council

Teneriffe House

37 Teneriffe Drive, Teneriffe

Design: William Henry Ellerker
Built: 1865, extended 1886, 1919

On the heights of the suburb of Teneriffe, evidence of the historic Teneriffe House is hard to see from the Brisbane River, however, the imposing bunya pine [*Araucaria bidwillii*] that stands across the street of this significant architectural site proves to be a powerful signpost to history. The gully at Beetson Street below Teneriffe House was a First Nations' burial area and dance ground.

14. Bulimba

Bulimba is a vast block of sandstone originally called *Toogoolawah* ('shaped like a heart'). With its Bay breezes and many micro-environments of wallum, swamp, and rainforest, it was a favourite camping ground for First Nations people. It had over 10 closely spaced camps and saw regular pademelon and bandicoot drives.

Children playing in the water next to the Oxford Street ferry terminal, Bulimba.
John Oxley Library

Bulimba Ferry Terminal

Oxford St, Bulimba

Built: 1922

The best example of an early ferry terminal can be viewed at the end of Oxford Street, Bulimba, and part of the rare adjacent vehicular roadway that was used to facilitate access to the steam vehicular ferry *Hetherington,* which travelled for many years between Commercial Road, Teneriffe and Oxford Street.

This is now a popular restaurant and venue strip.

Bulimba State School

271 Oxford St, Bulimba

Built: 1867, 1915, 1946

Bulimba State School, infants building, 1915.
Brisbane City Council

Behind the historic Bulimba ferry terminal, the suburb is crowned by the imposing Bulimba State School, which is a fine example of a between-the-wars education institution. A National School – forerunner of the Queensland State School – had been established in 1866 when it then was surrounded by a series of allotments where farmers raised livestock, dairy and agricultural produce.

The Bulimba State School would evolve in time such that, by 1938, the bulk of the structure visible today was *in situ*.

Bulimba State School, 1946.
Queensland State Archives

Bulimba House

34 Kenbury Street, Bulimba

Design: Andrew Petrie
Built: 1850

In the garden at Bulimba House, c. 1905.
John Oxley Library

Built in a style redolent of the kind of English country homes found in Kent, Bulimba was the residence of the pioneering McConnel family and, later on, residence of Queensland Premier AE Moore. Originally known as Toogoolawah. When built, the house was very isolated and surrounded by a patch of rainforest. For this reason, and because warrior-leaders such as Yilbung and Mulrobin often stayed nearby, the owners installed defensive louvred windows and kept guard dogs.

15. Teneriffe

Our Lady of Victories

1 Roche Ave, Bowen HIlls
Design: Messrs Hall and Prentice
Built: 1924

Our Lady of Victories Catholic Church at Bowen Hills, ca. 1928
John Oxley Library

The crest of the suburb of Bowen Hills is dominated by the steeple of Our Lady of Victories Roman Catholic Church, constructed between 1924 and 1925 as a memorial to Roman Catholic service personnel who had seen service in The Great War.

Designed in the Spanish mission style and built by H Cheetham at a cost of £9435, the Church is located on part of the old Folkestone Estate of William Perry.

Newstead House

Corner Newstead Ave and Breakfast Creek Road, Newstead

Design: Andrew Petrie

Built: 1846

Looking towards Newstead House from Breakfast Creek, c. 1918.
John Oxley Library

Newstead House is the oldest surviving home in Brisbane. The house was built as a small cottage for Patrick Leslie and later was extended by Captain John Wickham and then George Harris. Under Leslie and Wickham, Newstead House became the political and social hub of Brisbane – central to the debates that led to Queensland's Separation in 1859. The homestead of today embraces, cocoon-like, the original Newstead Cottage of 1846. Newstead House is open to the public.

Newstead House

Newstead Park

First Nations people knew this area and Newstead House as Garran-babilli. This referred to the vines that grew here, which were used for building. They used the rocks for spearfishing and the figs that grew on the lower slopes were where they interred some of the bones of their elders, tying them into the branches.

The current Park is the remnant of the grand estate of George Harris, merchant and United States Consul-General, and is home to several memorials – it is especially known for the Australian-American Memorial, erected in 1951 to honour the role of Americans in defending Australia during World War 2. The park is also home to the unique Tide Gauge, gift of the British India Steam Navigation Coy in Queensland's Centenary year 1959.

Hamilton Reach of the Brisbane River, c. 1912.
John Oxley Library

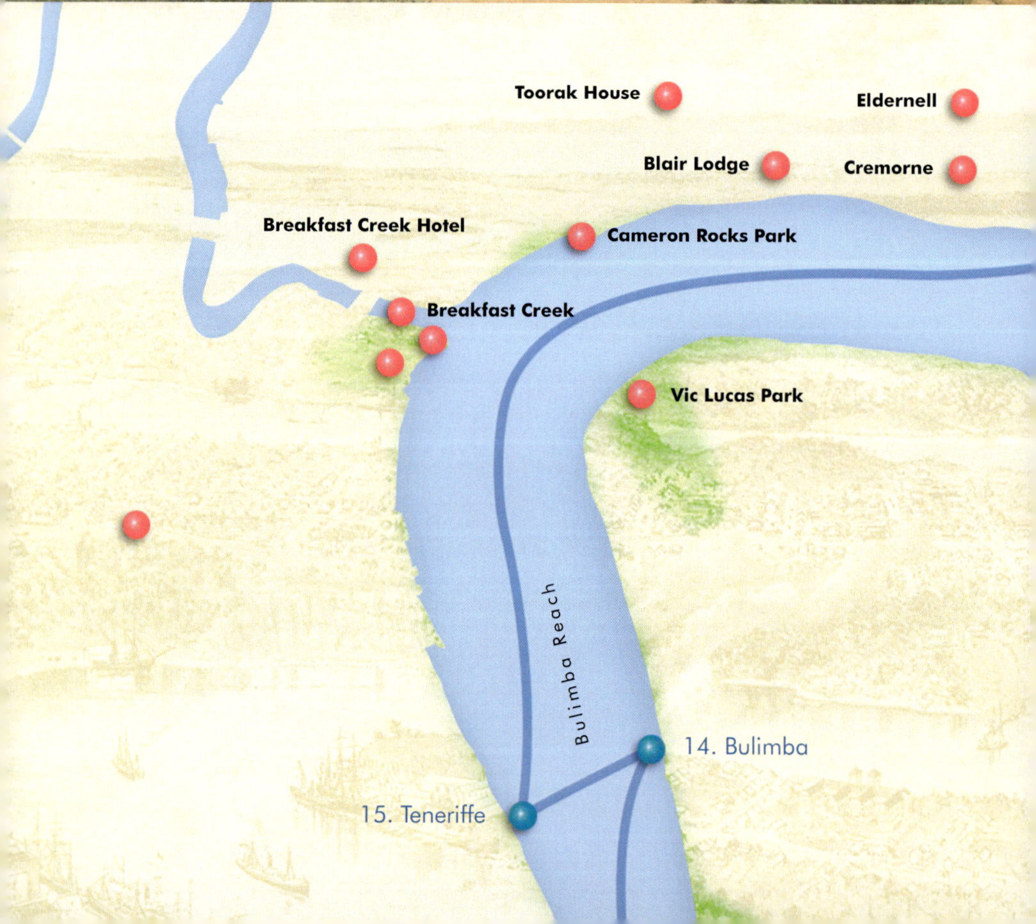

Toorak House

Eldernell

Blair Lodge

Cremorne

Breakfast Creek Hotel

Cameron Rocks Park

Breakfast Creek

Vic Lucas Park

Bulimba Reach

14. Bulimba

15. Teneriffe

Hamilton Reach

The Hamilton Reach of the Brisbane River marks what John Oxley (1823) called the end of the Great Sea Reach. During World War II this was a busy reach of the River. A large portion of the US Navy was for a while stationed here due to the efforts of the Pacific War – initially the Pensacola Convoy of December 1941 and the subsequent deployment of Ascot Racecourse as a camp for US military personnel.

Even earlier, and postwar, this reach welcomed rowers and regattas, which attracted huge crowds ,with many a house guest looking down from gracious homes such as Cremorne, Toorak House and Blair Lodge. It was also a place of 'promenading', with crowds in awe of the nautical gymnastics of the 16 and 18-footers.

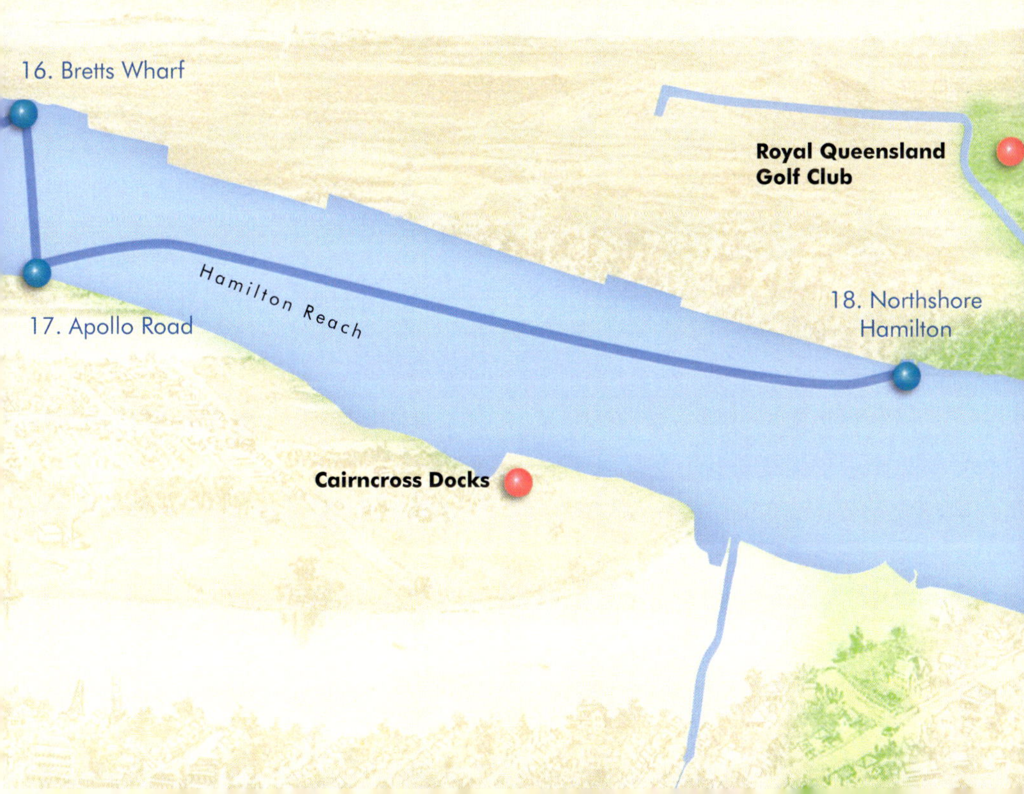

Hamilton Reach

Breakfast Creek

Breakfast Creek Bridge, c. 1889.
John Oxley Library

Breakfast Creek 'bookends' this reach of the river, a creek of two names – the first inspired by the fact that Messrs John Oxley, Allan Cunningham and Lieutenant Butler all took breakfast here in September 1824 – the second, the fact that the creek bordered by Bowen Bridge Road undergoes a name change to Enoggera Creek. *You-arr-garee* ('corroboree place/ place of waters') was the original name for the area around the creek mouth. It had six camps, which were several times attacked and burnt down between the 1840s and 1870s. From here, the headman Dalaipi composed his 'Indictments' – some of the earliest First Nations' writing.

Breakfast Creek Hotel

2 Kingsford-Smith Drive, Breakfast Creek

Design: Simkin and Ibler

Built: 1889

Floodwaters at the Breakfast Creek Hotel, 1893.

John Oxley Library

Inspired by a meandering Breakfast Creek (which curiously has a name change the further you travel beyond where the creek joins the Brisbane River), the present-day Breakfast Creek Hotel was constructed for William MacNaughton Galloway, seaman's outfitter and one-time Mayor of Brisbane. Built at a cost of £5300, it followed an earlier Breakfast Creek Hotel. The foundation stone to the present building dated from 18 May 1889, with the hotel opening for trading one year later on 17 May 1890, coinciding with the opening of a new bridge over Breakfast Creek.

Ⓝ Palma Rosa Residence

9 Queens Road, Hamilton

Design: Andrea Stombuco
Built: 1886-7

Nearby is the campus of the St Margaret's School, marked by examples of colonial architecture and mature trees fulfilling their role as 'Signposts to History', and nestling in the escarpment is the exuberant Andrea Stombuco's residence, Palma Rosa, formerly Sans Souci, now a private residence. This signature building with its soaring tower and three storeys was frequented by Brisbane Society and reports survive of race-day veranda parties when 'bookies' would visit the residence to take bets. In time the residence was converted into flats and a convalescence hospital before being purchased in 1972 by The English-Speaking Union which, in 2010, sold the building.

Back view of Palma Rosa at Hamilton.
John Oxley Library

Vic Lucas Park

On the other side of the river, it is a reminder of the halcyon days when 16-footers and 18-footers jostled for favourable wind in the many regattas conducted in the Hamilton Reach of the Brisbane River. This was an important traditional crossing point and some-time camp. It was also a point that was used to corral wallabies during inter-tribal hunting drives.

Cameron Rocks Reserve

Adjacent to where Toorak Road and Kingsford-Smith Drive join, it is named for the auctioneer Cameron who lived opposite the reserve; originally an important *pullen-pullen* (Aboriginal tournament ground) and a fishing ground for catching bream. Cameron Rocks was also the site of the Salvation Army Maternity Home in the early 1900s. Many First Nations families connected to the Brisbane and Sunshine Coast regions had an ancestor residing here. Aboriginal unionist Des Donley (1914–2011) was born at this Home. It was later site of a war memorial acknowledging those from the surrounding district who served in conflict.

Cameron Rocks Reserve

Toorak House

28 Annie Street, Hamilton

Built: c. 1865, extended 1890s

In any telling of the stories of this reach of the Brisbane River it would be remiss not to mention Brisbane's equivalent of a 'castle', Toorak House providing an architectural ornament on another of the hills within the ridge. This residence, complete with turret, was erected for businessman James Robert Dickson, who in time would become Premier of Queensland (1898-99) and, later still, the first Commonwealth Minister for Defence in the Barton Government post-Federation. Later still, from 1907 through 1910, the residence underwent a name change, becoming the Eton High School (the forerunner of the St Margaret's School of today at nearby Albion). The site was originally one of the Breakfast Creek Aboriginal camps. It had several native (rock) wells.

Dickson family, Toorak House, Brisbane, 1872.
John Oxley Library

Toorak House, Hamilton, Brisbane c. 1870.
John Oxley Library

Blair Lodge

Kingsford-Smith Drive

Design: Claude William Chambers
Built: 1912

Kingsford-Smith Drive, c. 1912.
Detail. Blair Lodge in the foreground.
John Oxley Library

Closer to the water's edge and busy Kingsford-Smith Drive is the Claude Chambers-designed home Blair Lodge. With its exquisite architectural trappings it is the personification of the Federation house. Chambers was one of this City's most celebrated and sought-after architects.

Bishopbourne, formerly Eldernell

39 Eldernell Terrace, Hamilton

Design: James Cowlishaw
Built: 1869

Hamilton residence Eldernell.
John Oxley Library

Another also visible homestead is on the ridge above the river. This is Eldernell, which was constructed for the Hemmant Family. Two Aboriginal camps were once on this location – one towards the hill slope – which were both destroyed by police in 1861. It could also quite legitimately be called a 'palace', serving as the home of the Archbishop of Brisbane from 1964 to 2007.

Eldernell front gate today

Among gracious residences observing this reach is Cremorne, which was constructed for the publican Denis O'Connor and readily noticed through its use of timber, tin, veranda pavilions and garden plantings.

Ⓝ Cremorne House

34 Mullens Street, Hamilton

Design: Eaton & Bates

Built: 1905–6

Cremorne residence on Hamilton Hill, c. 1906.
John Oxley Library

16. Bretts Wharf

Bretts Wharf at Hamilton, ca. 1929.
John Oxley Library

The largest First Nations' camp of the lower Brisbane area was located here. It stretched from Bretts Wharf and along the river, running beside the former sand spit of *Mooroo-Mooroolbin* ('place of the long-nose' – the ibis – the spit being also shaped like an ibis head). This was a vital net-fishing spot during the annual mullet run. Being so close to Kingsford Smith Drive (originally an Aboriginal Pathway), it was also an area of much conflict with settlers. During World War II this was a busy reach of the River... initially the Pensacola convoy of December 1941 and the subsequent deployment of Ascot Racecourse as a camp for US military personnel.

US Army transport ship *Republic* arriving in Brisbane with the Pensacola convoy, 1 December 1941.
John Oxley Library

Hamilton Cold Stores and wharf, c. 1927.
John Oxley Library

17. Apollo Road

The Apollo (named for the one-time Apollo Candle Company) Barge Assembly Depot, USAOS was the site of a couple of First Nations camps, whose members would regularly help haul barges across between here and Brett's Wharf. In the 1880s-1890s, the Candle Factory served as a reformatory training centre for Aboriginal and other youth, but the area is best known as the naval base – where members of the Chinese community were engaged building barges for the Pacific War, one of whom being the distinguished late Brisbane identity Eddie Liu OBE, OAM. In 1944, some 300 of these Chinese workers rioted, resulting in 11 injuries and a subsequent murder.

Apollo Road factory

Cairncross Docks

405 Thynne Road, Morningside

The Cairncross Rocks were probably once a Dreaming site, as the area (called *Tintahmpa*) had a corroboree ground and a women's burial ground. The women were interred in bark wrappings, in the forks of trees. Cairncross Dock has fallen silent for the moment, however, it has shown its resilience to the winds of economic change. The first docking occurred in June 1944 when Brisbane was very much a 'garrison city', with an official opening on 16 September 1944. The dock closed in 1987 and reopened on 3 August 1995 with the name and location of 'Cairncross' attributed to a feature of the south side of the Brisbane River called Cairncross Rocks, while in turn it had taken its name from a successful Brisbane businessman in the 1840s, William Cairncross, who built Colmslie House at Bulimba.

Cairncross dock site, c. 1949.
Queensland State Archives

18. Northshore Hamilton

Northshore Recreation Park

This new residential development called Northshore was originally a rainforest pocket called *Yurrol* (the name of a climbing vine). It consisted of cedars, yellow wood, figs, cabbage tree palms and black bean. Today it is a mix of recreational space, apartments and riparian art with a beach. It is serviced by a CityCat terminal. The distinctive paving surrounding the onsite restaurant (in its cocoon of award-winning bronze sculpture) tells the story of the Brisbane River through 'moments in its history'.

Across the river is the Raptis Fish Market.

Royal Queensland Golf Club

431 Curtin Avenue West, Eagle Farm

Founded: 1920

Royal Queensland Golf Club, home of three Australian Open Championships. The Club covers part of the former Yurrol rainforest. Granted its Royal Charter in 1921, Royal Queensland was described as 'an excellent test of golf' by the famous Scots golf course architect Dr Alister MacKenzie, who visited in 1926. The decision to build a parallel bridge to augment what are now called the Heilscher Bridges cost the RQGC seven holes, causing the reconfiguration of the golf course.

About the Author

David Gibson (deceased) was synonymous with the history of Brisbane. As a professional historian and commentator for over 35 years, David believed our past is alive and reflected in our uniquely built environment; seen in our memorials and in the efforts of historical societies and associations and in the actions of individuals who seek to place the past before the widest possible community.

David was an Honours Graduate from the University of Queensland. His areas of research and interest were in Australian Federation history; Australia's maritime heritage; the Pitcairners, descendants of the mutineers of HMAV *Bounty*; Napoleon Bonaparte; the voyages of HMS *Beagle*; the prominent designer of the Victorian Period AWN Pugin, the House of Plantagenet and of course, Brisbane.

David served as a member of the John Oxley Library Advisory Committee, the Queensland working party of *The Australian Dictionary of Biography*, the Executive of the National Trust of Queensland and including a member of the Friends of Newstead Inc. In 1988 he received the Norfolk Island Bicentenary Medal for his work in promoting the conservation values of this most important historic precinct and was invited to present the Macrossan Lecture in the refurbished Customs House upon its acquisition by the University of Queensland. In 2002, David was the keynote speaker at the Henry Parkes Banquet in the historic School of Arts building in Tenterfield.

Within the Museums and Gallery sector, David served as President of the Queensland branch of Museums Australia and spent time on the judging and advisory panels of the GAMMAS – awards honouring excellence by organisations and individuals within the museum and gallery sector in Queensland. He participated as an advisor in the 'Standards' Programme organised by M&GSQ and was an advisor to the Queensland Government on the development of the Queensland Heritage Trails. David was an inaugural member of the committee that established Brisbane's Living Heritage.

David had a deep and proven commitment to the 'bringing to life' the cultural landscape at every opportunity. David was also a regular contributor to the *History Queensland* magazine, published quarterly in Queensland, and conducted South East Queensland Heritage workshops and tours to places of historic importance.